Lorrie Panzeri

Lorrie Panzeri has worked in healthcare for over twenty years. She has been blessed to work as a Community Liaison in the home health and hospice arena for the past ten years. She enjoys meeting with families and sharing the gift of hospice with those in need.

At the tender age of four her granddaughter, Payton asked a simple question, "Nana, what would happen if you died?" The result of that question is this book, eight years later!! Lorrie's hope is that this book will touch the lives of families and give them comfort.

Lorrie is passionate about writing and believes that if a child's feelings are validated then they will feel safe and loved. Isn't that what we all want in life? Touch a child's life with love and you have experienced how to live life to the fullest.

I dedicate this book to my granddaughter Payton Panzeri. Because of her love and curiosity this book will help other children in time of sorrow. Because of you we will be able help children get through one of the hardest parts in life we all come to experience, a death. God bless you sweet girl. I love you "disssss much"!
Nana Lorrie

Karen Martinat

Karen Martinat is a Licensed Clinical Social Worker who specializes in spiritual well-being, trauma and grief. She has over seventeen years' experience working with patients and families who are dealing with the intimate end-of-life process. She understands the unique needs of children and hopes this book will be instrumental in helping a child through the journey of grief. Karen enjoys spending time with her family and friends in southern Idaho and can often be found on the majestic Salmon River during Steel-head season. Karen Martinat is a Certified Laughter Yoga Instructor and understands the therapeutic benefit of laughter during difficult times.

I dedicate this book to my sons, Jacob and Nicholas and my adventuresome grandsons' Danny, Carter and Emmett. I love you to the moon and back!

Scott Pentzer

Scott Pentzer has been an artist since he was a child. He grew up reading comic books and idolizing comic book artist's. He moved from Lewiston, Idaho to Boise, Idaho in 1984 to attend Boise State University where he majored in Art. He began to do freelance illustration professionally in 1989. He has worked with many Idaho advertising agencies as an illustrator and as a storyboard artist. He did the final illustration for the Idaho Ski License Plate. He went on to draw many comic books for various companies over the years and has also worked directly for the legendary rock band KISS. Scott has three children of his own and two stepchildren. He spends most of his time being a father and some of his time drawing.

I Miss My Nana
Copyright © 2016 by Lorrie Panzeri & Karen Martinat

Warning: The unauthorized reproduction or distribution of this copyrighted work is illegal. Criminal copyright infringement, including infringement without monetary gain, is investigated by the FBI and is punishable by up to 5 (five) years in federal prison and a fine of $250,000.

Names, characters and incidents depicted in this book are products of the author's imagination or are used fictitiously. Any resemblance to actual events, locales, organizations, or persons, living or dead, is entirely coincidental and beyond the intent of the author or the publisher.

No part of this book may be reproduced or transmitted in any form or by any means, electronic or mechanical, including photocopying, recording, or by any information storage and retrieval system, without permission in writing from the author.

Art: Scott E. Pentzer

I Miss My Nana

Written by:
Lorrie Panzeri
&
Karen Martinat, LCSW

Illustrated by:
Scott Pentzer

Intended to help children in
dealing with the death of
a loved one.

My Nana is the bestest Nana in the whole wide world! She gives me lots of hugs and kisses all the time. She tickles me until I get the giggles. Nana laughs when I get the giggles. I love to make her laugh.

Mommy told me that Nana is not feeling good and that we should go visit her a lot more and tell her how much we love her.

I love going to Nana's house because we do lots of fun things together. I wish I could help Nana feel better. Mommy says she is going to die and go to heaven. Sometimes people get sick and don't get better.

Mommy says heaven is a beautiful place where we go to live with God. Mommy says there is no sickness in heaven and that there are beautiful angels there!!

Mommy says...I have lots of special memories about Nana and I can keep them safe in my heart forever. I like to call her "Nana Banana". She thinks that is funny and always smiles when I call her that name.

I like to spend the night with Nana. I take my favorite blanket so she can read to me until I fall asleep. Mommy says Nana will be taking more naps now and that I can still snuggle with her.

Nana knows how to make the bestest cookies ever! She lets me crack the eggs and helps me mix up the other stuff in the bowl so we can bake them. They smell so good when she takes them out of the oven. They taste yummy for our tummy!

Decorate this COOKIE the way you want...

I get to decorate the cookies with fun colors and sprinkles. I try to paint rainbows on top of the cookies. Sometimes mine look like a bunch of crazy mixed up colors, but Nana doesn't mind. She says that cookies taste good no matter how the frosting looks!

We like to pop popcorn and watch fun movies together! She laughs and cries at the same times I do. It makes me feel happy that I am like her.

Sometimes when it is warm outside we plant flowers. We both love the color purple. Nana is pretty like the flowers.

**This page is for YOU to COLOR!

Nana loves to play dress up maybe even more than me! We have tea parties in our dress up clothes and eat the rainbow cookies.

We love to listen to music together. Nana dances silly and so do I. We laugh so much that it makes our tummies hurt.

**This page is for YOU to COLOR!

We love to color. Nana can stay in the lines. She teaches me to stay in the lines and likes the colors I use in the crayon box.

**This page is for YOU to COLOR!

Sometimes I feel sad when I think of what Mommy said about Nana dying and going to heaven. I want her to stay with me, but Nana isn't going to get better.

After Nana died we went to her funeral. We had to say goodbye to her. Mommy says it is okay to cry when I feel sad. I have lots of tears. Mommy does too. What will I do without my Nana? I am so sad. I will miss her so much.

Mommy told me we can remember Nana in our hearts forever because of all the memories stored there. Thinking about fun memories makes my heart not feel so sad.

Sometimes at night when the sky is dark and I look up to see the shining stars I know Nana is winking at me! She liked to wink at me when she was telling a story.

Mommy has lots of pictures of Nana in books that I get to look at. This helps me remember all the times Nana hugged, kissed, and tickled me. She will always be the bestest Nana in the whole wide world!

**Note to Readers: These spaces are for you to draw your favorite memories.

I say a prayer and thank the angels for watching over Nana. "Please take care of her for me. When she makes her special 'Nana cookies' in heaven, remember to tell her that they will be my favorite cookies, always!!"

Tips for Parents

The following activities are intended to assist you in helping your child work through their feelings associated with the death of a loved one. Children learn and process emotions through play. They are "hands-on" learners. The use of creative projects will provide the atmosphere for open/honest communication and allow your child to let you know what they need.

Young children do not always have the "words" to let you know what they are feeling; it is often acted out in play. We are all unique, wonderful beings that experience emotions in our own way - children are no exception. Their grief process will be unique to them. Some important things to remember are:

- Allow your child to lead the conversation - let them ask what they need to know.
- Keep your child's routine as normal as possible - they need to know they are safe and loved. Ask family and friends to assist with this. It is often very difficult to maintain "normal" routines when parents are processing their own grief.
- Always use "real" words such as dead, dying, etc. Refrain from words such as sleeping, gone to rest or passed on.
- Be honest with what you are feeling. If you need to cry that's "OK"...simply let your child know. "Mommy is feeling sad right now because she misses (insert loved ones name) and having tears helps me feel better." Reassure them that they are safe and loved. Children can feel when something is not right and trying to hide your emotions is very confusing for them.
- Seek help. Reach out to others who have shared a similar situation. Contact your local hospice for additional information on community resources.

Activities: Making "Nana" Cookies

Ingredients:

1 Cup Softened Butter
1 Teaspoon Vanilla
1 1/2 Cups White Sugar
2 3/4 Cups All-Purpose Flour
1 Teaspoon Baking Soda
1 Egg

Instructions:

1. Preheat Oven to 375 degrees F (190 degrees C). In a small bowl, stir together flour, baking soda and baking powder. Set aside.
2. In a large bowl, cream together the butter and sugar until smooth. Beat in egg and vanilla. Gradually blend in the dry ingredients. Roll rounded teaspoonful of dough into balls, and place onto ungreased cookie sheets.
3. Bake 8 to 10 minutes before removing to cool on wire rack.

Memory Popcorn

Materials Needed:

- Popcorn
- Silly Attitude

Instructions:

Set aside some time to laugh, be silly and talk about memories! Before each person can eat a piece of popcorn they need to share a memory about their loved one. Make sure to validate all emotions that arise.

Make a Memory Garden

Materials Needed:

- Seeds, plants, flowers
- Watering bucket
- Small shovel, spade, etc.
- Laminated picture of loved one attached to a Popsicle stick.

Instructions:

Being in nature and watching things grow is a wonderful way to allow your child to express their feelings or ask questions regarding the death. Allow your child to pick out the flowers and design the memory garden. If space or climate is an issue, you can always make a planting box.

Making a Memory Box

Materials Needed:

- Shoe box
- Glue, scissors
- Colored paper, crayons and markers.
- Stickers, glitter, yarn
- Pictures (color copies work great)

Instructions:

Explain to your child that they are going to make a very special memory box. Assist them with decorating outside of the box with pictures, stickers, yarn, etc. Then have them place items inside the box that hold special memories. Let your child find the "perfect place" to display the memory box. This activity is a wonderful way to assist your child in sharing their story and honoring memories.

Feeling Masks

Materials Needed:

- Paper plates
- Glue, scissors, hole-punch
- Colored paper, crayons, markers
- Stickers, glitter, yarn

Instructions:

Making feeling masks will help you understand the varied feelings that children often exhibit when dealing with loss. Allow your child to draw a face that looks happy, sad, scared or mad, or whatever they are feeling. Hole punch on both sides and attach yarn.

Possible conversation starters, "Sometimes we have worried feelings, or thoughts or questions or even nightmares. They stay inside us and we don't know whether to talk about them or not." Allow your child to lead the discussion as they put on each mask and act out the feeling.

www.ingramcontent.com/pod-product-compliance
Lightning Source LLC
Chambersburg PA
CBHW061402090426
42743CB00002B/109